BENEATH THE
SHADE

BENEATH THE SHADE

*the poetic self-discoveries and realizations
of a fellow human*

BY
PEARL-CATHERINE TITA

Beneath The Shade
Pearl-Catherine Tita

All rights reserved
First Edition, 2021
© Pearl-Catherine Tita, 2021
Cover art by: Olga Fedorets

No part of this publication may be reproduced, or stored in a retrieval system, or transmitted in any form by means of electronic, mechanical, photocopying or otherwise, without prior written permission from the author.

ISBN:-978-1-7776606-0-4

HI, I'M PEARL-CATHERINE.

Existing used to be easier when I was ignorant (well…at least I thought). The overwhelming truths of humanity did not negatively impact the mind of someone who was too young to *even care* to understand. I yearned for the independence that accompanied adulthood, now I crave the innocence that preceded it. I have been educated and I am grateful for knowledge. However, I despise this information. I have discovered that strategically hidden are fictitious events; fabrications that have been formulated to control the souls of the desperate. Along with lies that encapsulate the thoughts of the narrow-minded; of those who do not care to know better. I used to bask in my ignorance; I enjoyed seeking refuge in Lala Land. But currently I sit here writing—informed, nervous, and sure of only one thing that I want out of my existence…and that is to interlace my thought processes with yours.

What is your introduction?

Think about your daily transfers and exchanges of energy with those around you. When your name leaves the lips of another human, what defining words or phrases do you feel would follow? These descriptions in which YOU have thought of…are they in alignment with how you TRULY convey yourself to your fellow residents of Earth?

Simply for a few minutes, or however long it may take, be honest with yourself and answer this:

WHO THE FUCK ARE YOU?

Take the time to answer that question before you continue to read. Engage in some moments of introspection and take notes on the following page about your inner discoveries. Introspection consists of a deep self-analysis of your thoughts, emotions and actions. Bring your deepest fears, discomforts, and desires to the surface. Try to work through the difficulties and manifest the positives into the physical world. This may be intimidating to do if you have never really taken the time to deeply analyze your mind. Essentially, try your best to truly understand yourself.

My Inner Discoveries

Finally, this book is a compilation of poems in which I have written over several years. Some of these poems have been re-written many times, as they have transformed with me while I journey through life. These are the inner workings of my brain for you to read. I truly hope these resonate with you <3

your transparency
may be the source
of someone's awakening
p.c.

INTROSPECTING

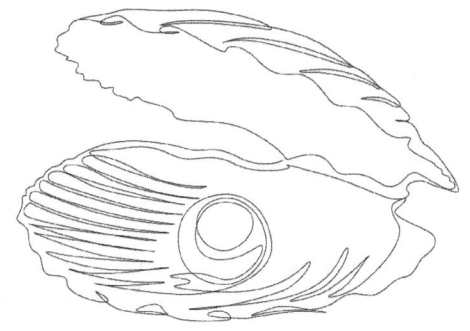

in the stillness;
only in the most serene
of environments
can an oyster produce
the most valued component
of its existence.

pearl.

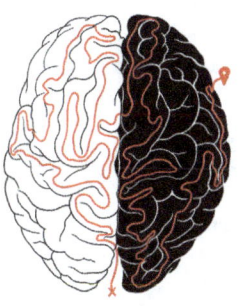

canvassing your thoughts;
exploring the dark burrows
of your mind
can be intimidating.
the fear of evoking memories
which have been dormant for years
is not irrational,
but you want to continue
to keep a peaceful mind.
so you continue to suppress
for the sake of your well-being.
but you are also obsessive;
….so you continue to explore
and find what you didn't want to.

enter at your own risk.

everything
about who you are,
before you knew
who you were;
exists within the confines
of your physical being.
venture inward;
embrace the stillness
of isolation
and find solace
within the intricacies
of your individuality.
….familiarize yourself
with yourself.

soulitary confinement.

she was choosing not to drown
in the high-frequency beta waves
emitted by her brain
as she swam amongst
the depths of her consciousness;
in search of the beauty
in understanding
her characteristic flaws.

without a life jacket.

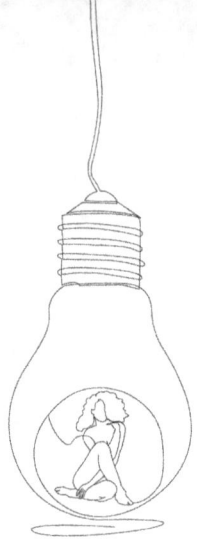

we visit dark places
often by ourselves,
so others wouldn't know
about our daily visits.
it is in these moments of darkness
where there is no difference;
between eyes wide open
or tightly shut…
your retinas adjusting
to the absence of hope.

insufficient lighting.

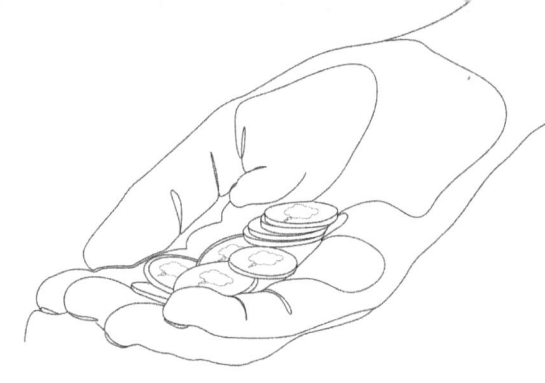

clarity is what the mind craves
when it is constantly fed
with information of your
inabilities and inadequacies;
which are reinforced
by your struggles
and questionable failures.
concern of your earthly contributions
is the spine
of your inquisitiveness.
the act of wondering
is your most hated
yet,
time consuming pastime.
you hunger for clarity;
but you are a few cents short
of what it costs to know
….so you rummage.

spare change?

i didn't know
where my mind
was taking me,
but i knew
i no longer
belonged here.

realization.

pack up your heaviest thoughts
and catch the next flight
to infinity.
do not return
until you have located
your serenity.

ticket for one.

you thought it would be easy
to remove yourself
from the vulnerable space;
where insecurities formulate
emotional catastrophes.
but you have equated
what you think is love
with a vital organ;
misinformed that your survival
is contingent
upon one word;
you must relinquish yourself
of the tendency
to be weak-minded.

the great escape.

LETTING A STRANGER IN

presently,
she wished to be in his presence.
….wanting to bask in his energy;
no romantic shit…
just looking to absorb the positive vibes
he would emit.

vibration mode: ON.

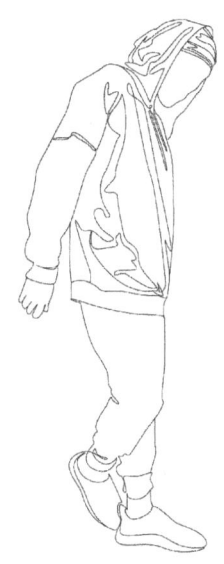

what intrigued her
was his silence;
everyone was not deserving
of the vocalization
of his thought processes.

mute.

i tried to resist
the newness
of foreign skin
but,
i adored your hues.
undertone;
like the inside
of a partially ripened mango
lips like papaya
eyes like the shell of a coconut;
my caribbean boy.

gwannn beautiful king.

i experience
vacations with you
though,
we have yet
to cross borders together.

my sunshine, my getaway.

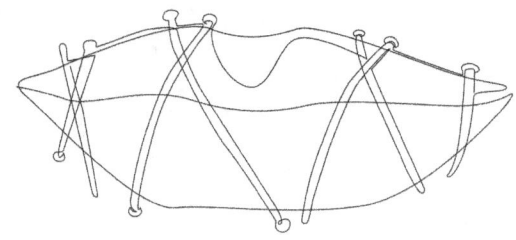

with the absence
of words,
communicate to me.

language of the body.

inhabitants of the 3rd planet from the sun;
the souls of 2 human beings
coming together as 1.

countdown to romantic love.

we lay;
staring into quiet eyes
holding each other's deepests,
from our darkest
of times.

telepathic communication.

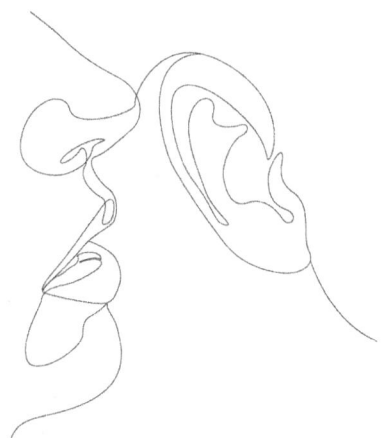

i want the tiny bones
in your middle ear
to experience the vibrations
from my vocal cords
when i am finally able to formulate
the syllables of that one letter
and two words;
enunciated by the positions
of my tongue
against the structures
of my mouth.

                                                    i love you.

draped in your mela-linen
you would hold me;
keeping me warm
amongst the luxury
of your earth tones.

skin so rich.

days spent with you
felt like hours,
hours spent with you
felt like minutes,
but time spent without you
felt…. too long.

the illusion.

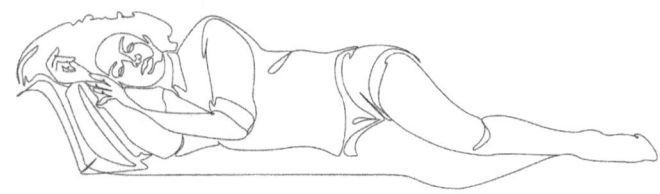

i never had trouble
sleeping alone;
i looked forward to sharing my bed
with my laptop.
but now you'd share your bed with me;
your head laying
in my lap
or my head laying
on your chest.
your sleeping face
in my lips' reach
i whisper "i love you"
not knowing if you loved me;
but hoping that you would
eventually.
i now had trouble sleeping
when i returned to my place of residence.
i had enjoyed a bed with no vacancy,
now mine needed an occupant.

vacancy; one spot left.

he was constantly
the subject
of the 1:00 am class
that she would attend
every night
in her head.

B+ student.

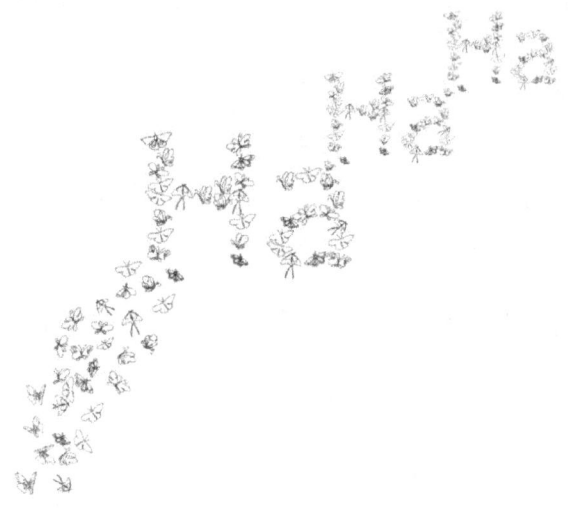

listening
to his laugh
would become the technique
that grounded her.

attributions.

that moment
when you no longer "like"
but "love"
no longer "want"
but "need"
it's no longer "i"
but "us";
that's the moment when security
is transformed to vulnerability.
you are now easily susceptible
to false realities
and illusions of tranquility.
your selflessness;
involuntary.
their well-being
is now your number one priority.

> *a slave to the hormonal*
> *functions of your pituitary.*

perfection
is not what i've looked for,
nor is it what i've found.
never sought this love either,
but found it in the most
imperfect way.
through hardships and tears
was how i came to love
an imperfect being…
who in return,
has learned to love
an imperfect me.

unexpected.

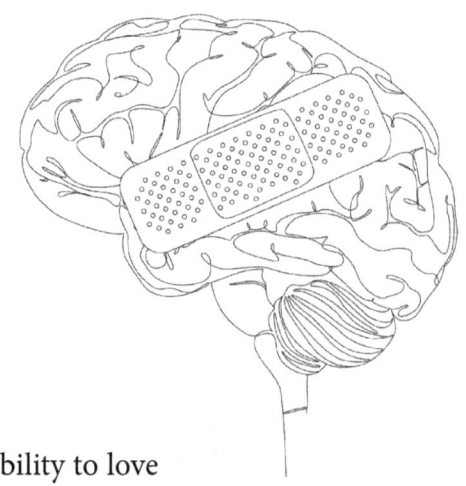

i let you see my scars;
my mental disfigurations
manifested into my incapability to love
…me.
i revealed the tools
that i used to build my wall,
you gave me the tools
to break it down.
my scars would no longer be hidden
but acknowledged
and explained.
i would abandon my insecurities
and allow serenity to flourish
in this once
dimly
lit
space.

renovating.

in experiencing the same thing
differently;
she thought it was more
…he knew it wasn't.
love didn't live in his house
like it did
within the temporal lobe of her brain.
he catered to the gratification
of her emotions
though,
sexual gratification
was all he sought.
this would conflict with her inability
to dissociate sex and love.

miscommunication 101.

REGRETTING OPENING THE DOOR

naïve;
i handed some parts of me
to a handsome being
who would tip my crown
instead of fixing it.

jester.

why was i constantly digging;
searching to find
the kindness
which i believed
lay dormant
beneath your hardened exterior?
this was supposed to be love,
…not a treasure hunt.

x.

she took proclamations of love
for face value
although,
there was no value
in his actions.
words so meaningful
made meaningless
by a self-serving
asshole;
creating an inner turmoil
between what she wanted
and what she should have known
she did not need.

dissonance.

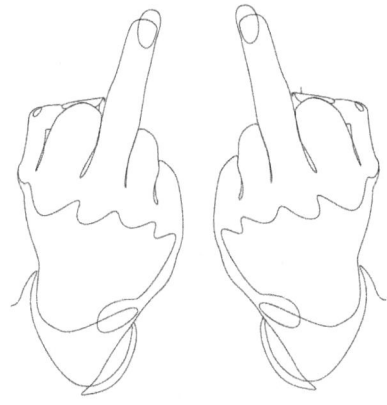

wannabe-soulful beings
simply…
so full of shit.

see-through.

where there is no logic,
stupidity manifests.

duh.

he recited lyrics
of a song
that she thought
hadn't been written;
an original piece
being composed
for her heart
only.
however,
she would be devastated
when she heard
those lyrics
leaving female lips;
that were not
her own.

she thought it was a duet, not a trio.

have you ever been told
that you were loved,
but the sentence that preceded
was that he was in love
with his past?
so… he loves you too.
…he loves you two.

fuck boy shit.

you were once
a breath of fresh air
until you polluted
my life,
tainted
my mind;
with insecurities
i never knew existed.
our coexistence
would now
make it hard
for me to breathe.

suffocate.

she composed a letter
that she would
tear up
and re-write
one hundred times.
she teared up;
knowing that she
was willingly refusing
to meet the requirements
of a position that she felt
once suited her.
she would hand the man
who once held her heart,
her resignation letter
from love.

permanently clocking out.

the memories
of a person she loved,
would make her hate
her favourite love songs.

playlist deleted.

it sucks
when you have plans
for your future
laid out before you;
like an outfit
you're excited to wear.
but then you put that shit on
and it looks as stupid as
"he will change" sounds
leaving your mouth.

girl… just change clothes and go.

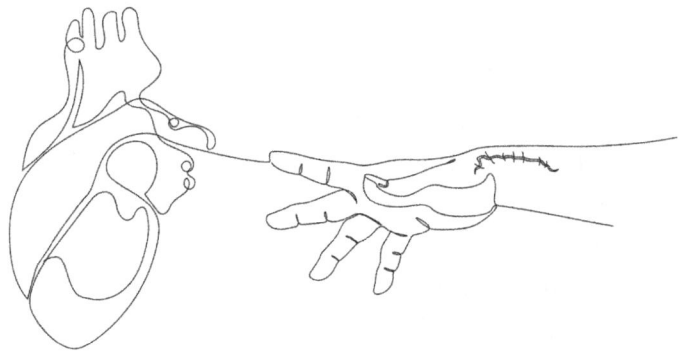

love;
doesn't expect you to adapt
to undesirable qualities.
however,
we adapt for the sake of love.

the tolerable heart.

i was unaware
of the fault in the lock.
i didn't understand
how you got in
however,
i still welcomed you;
my unwanted guest.
i was unaware
of the fault in the lock;
you infiltrated my soul
but i didn't
turn you away.
i led you into a room;
mislabeled boxes
containing all that i was
were stacked
pushed over
upside down
and crushed.
we bore witness to the mess
only for a moment,
then i asked you to leave.
i now had to find
a new lock
and i'd throw away
the key.

locksmith.

my mistake
was that i didn't
allow myself
the opportunity
to experience loneliness.
i learned that
humans are innately social,
but i needed to learn
to find strength
in *being able* to be alone.
so now i'm here;
unable to deal
with being alone
due to lack of experience.

newly single life lessons.

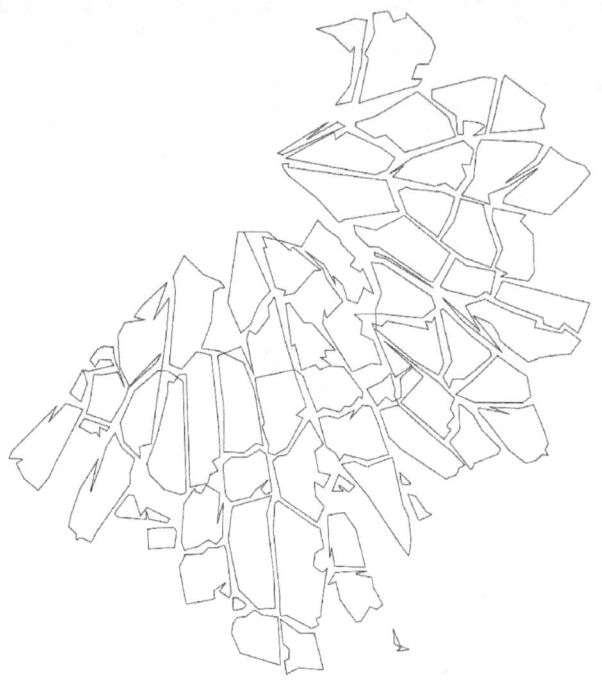

the belief
that we were meant to be,
would ruin
our realities.

definitely delusional.

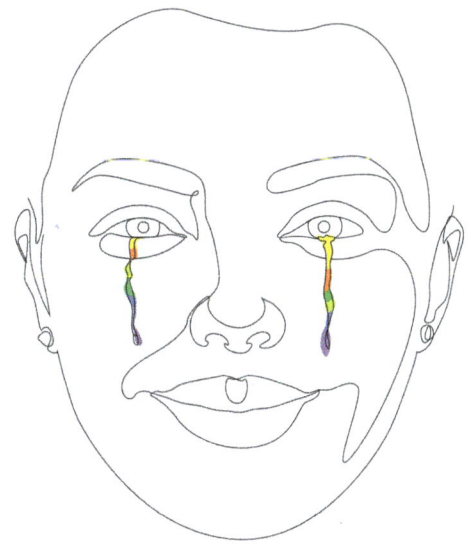

let your tears
just temporarily
stain your face,
not taint your heart.

no grudge zone.

GETTING IT TOGETHER

self-preservation
is instinctual;
but don't let fear
hold you back
from embarking on explorations
that surpass the perceived limitations
of your existence.

the scary leap of faith.

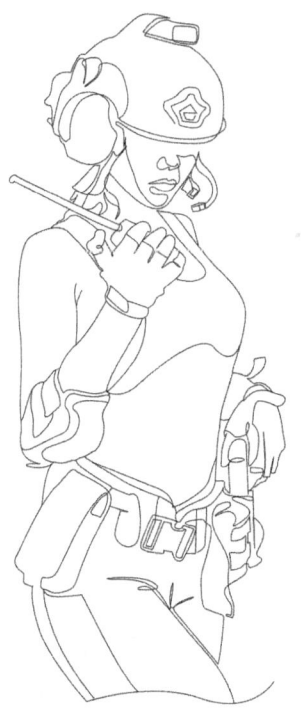

frontline of fears;
demolished.
stable frame of mind;
accomplished.
much damage done,
but the internal warfare
between prior and current self
has been won.

soldier.

in fear
of having to start over,
i almost missed out
on happiness.

tabula rasa.

for too many years
i have watched the snow melt,
the geese would come home,
and the smog alerts announced.
then the leaves would fall,
and the snow would return,
and i would remain
inexcusably unchanged.

be like the seasons.

plant your seeds
and let the bullshit
nourish your crops.

*kinda like that thing they say
about lemons and lemonade.*

do not put
the responsibility
of supporting your dreams
on anyone
but yourself.

dodgeball to the disappointments.

the processes of transformation
are not always clear.
growth is not immediate.
strength is progressively acquired;
through undergoing
and overcoming hardships.

have faith in the process.

yes,
 it still hurts
 …but you're healing.

the simple optimist.

let their lack of motivation,
become motivational.

unconventionally inspired.

reason will advise
that you shouldn't.
desperation will claim
that you won't survive without it.
but let resilience remind you;
you were born into this,
not born like this.
so stop being a dumbass
stop making bitch ass excuses
and decide to be great.

period.

be driven
by their doubt;
prove yourself
right.

nba 2019 champs!

AWARENESS

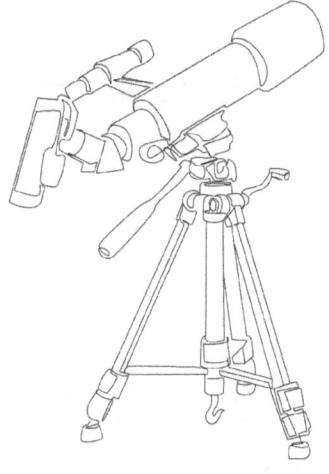

consciousness
intrinsic to our being;
has enabled our abilities
to innocently wonder
about the twinkle
of the little star,
and to brilliantly create
the technologies to explain
its existence.

the spectrum of a species.

have you ever pondered reality?
wondered how you could just trust…
that you're not being deceived
by your;
eyes
ears
nose
tongue
and
somatosensory system?
how can we be sure
of a true reality
when everyone's reality
is subjective?
no two people
will ever experience
their existences equally,
because of the discrepancies
in our being.
we do not experience
the world directly;
it is translated to us
through our senses,
and made sense by our brains.
so we are left only
with ideas
of what exists around us…

psychology lecture and plato got me thinking.

when consciousness
is restored,
and my subjective
perception of reality
is reintroduced;

by the adjustment of my pupils to the light,
an itch from dehydrated skin,
the tone of a text notification,
the bitterness of a rested tongue,
and the stench of morning's
first conscious breath;

…i know i'm awake.
well…
at least i think i am.

because the rough ledge
i was hanging from
8 seconds ago…
the exchange of frustration
that preceded the push;
well…
i'm surprised my consciousness
was restored;
that i'm back
to where repercussions
are tangible and permanent.

trying to make sense of my senses.

my eyelids;
the curtains to my
visual perceptions of the world
are closed.
i feel relieved;
for these moments
i'm no longer forced
to perceive the alterations
of self-regarding beings;
who have systematically
eradicated this ecosystem's authenticity.
so i keep my eyelids shut;
freeing my occipital lobe
of disappointments,
slowly distancing
myself from reality,
and escaping the mental adversities
of tangible images.

free blackout curtains.

human beings' discoveries
have simultaneously
made us aware
of the significance of our home,
and its insignificance
in the boundlessness
of the cosmos.

"the anthropology of outer space".

tap into your unawareness;
through discussions
of existence transcending physicality.
be liberated from your senses;
immerse yourself
into the incomprehensible
realization that reality
is in fact subjective.

metaphysical journey.

imagination
has temporarily filled voids;
enhancing curiosity
and fuelling our desire
to explore;
to seek out worlds
that were once conceived
only in our imaginations.

voyagers.

IMPERMANENCE

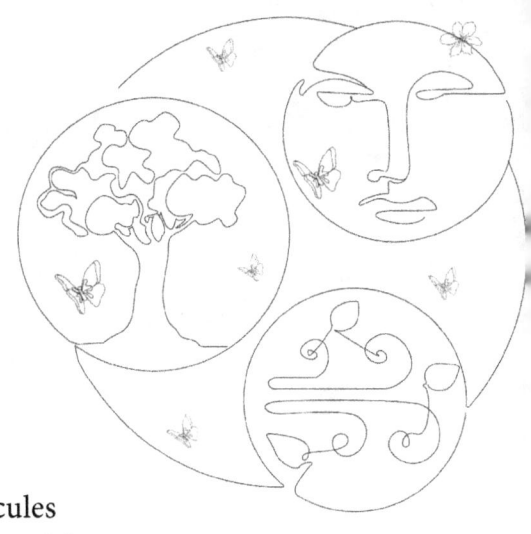

capitalize;
on every valuable
exchange of molecules
between your internal functions,
and the external doings
of nature.
for the primary confirmation
of life outside of the womb;
carbon dioxide's departure
and oxygen's arrival;
which feeds the internal
mechanisms of beings
who are raised to take
their being for granted…
is not deserved.

breathing is a privilege from God.

they hold notions
of the actions of brown skinned humans.
they hold guns
like babies held by mothers;
tightly,
many men
will never be held again.
they held him down
as he tried to hold
onto his last breath.
empty hands held high
to signify compliance;
too often has not been enough.
broken families
trying to hold things together.
women left holding down
single parent households
while holding back tears;
trying to uphold visuals
of strength for the kids.
yet the ones who held the gun
who held down the trigger
who held their knee
on the neck of the defenseless
are yet to be held accountable
for their actions.

g.f.

our time here,
is as temporary as the tears
embedded in the stitching of my shirt
as water molecules.
they will evaporate;
serving my soul a purpose
before they vanish.

what will be your purpose?

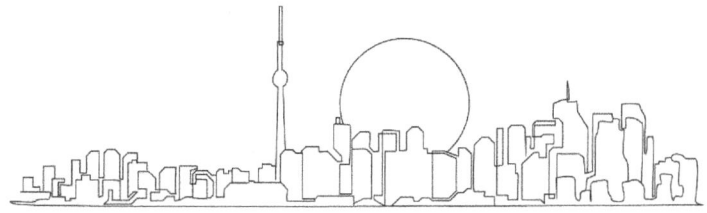

even if you miss
the introduction of the sun;
be in attendance
for the rest of nature's performances.
sit front and centre
at the orchestra of
storm clouds brewing,
harmonize with the voices
of the wind,
and be taken
by the choreography
of rain drops
dancing on the concrete.
for when the sun
takes its bow
and the curtains close…
you never know
if that would have been
your last show.

be present.

don't only cherish moments
because you think,
those will be the last moments
you'll be able to cherish.

rest in peace uncle O, forgive me.

THE SUM OF ALL THE PARTS

she would finally understand
that life was not linear;
finding comfort
in knowing
that she was simply blessed
to be able to walk
its crooked paths.

one step at a time.

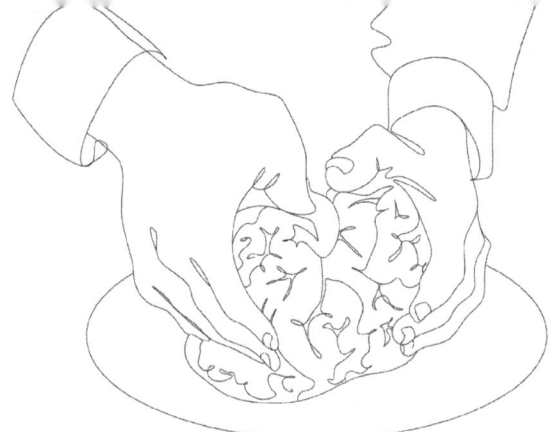

i once allowed myself
to be grasped
by the hands of society.
becoming easily manipulated
like clay;
they molded me
into their own image;
creating a misrepresentation
of what i was conceived to be.
i would experience
uncontrollable rise and falls
in my self-esteem;
because,
society held the remote
to my being.

the malleable mind.

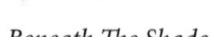

validation seekers;
i present myself to you
unbiased,
open-minded,
and regarding of your
innate failure to resist adherence
to dominant ideologies,
and empathetic
to your struggle for conformity.
validation seekers;
your strive for acceptance
from beings
who barely value themselves
is demeaning to
the authenticity of your existence.
validation seekers;
…accept yourselves.
fall in love
with the gap in your teeth
the discoloration of your skin.
the only validation you need
is within;
the departure of carbon dioxide
and the intake of oxygen
from your functioning lungs.
it's within;

the arteries carrying blood from
your beating organ
to the tips of your fingers
and soles of your feet.
breathe…
put your palm
over the left side
of your chest
and accept...
you.

seek no validation.

be the person
that your past self
would be excited to meet.

warm greetings.

true freedom:
is the emancipation
from the thoughts
that had held hostage
and captivated
your essence.

liberation never felt so good.

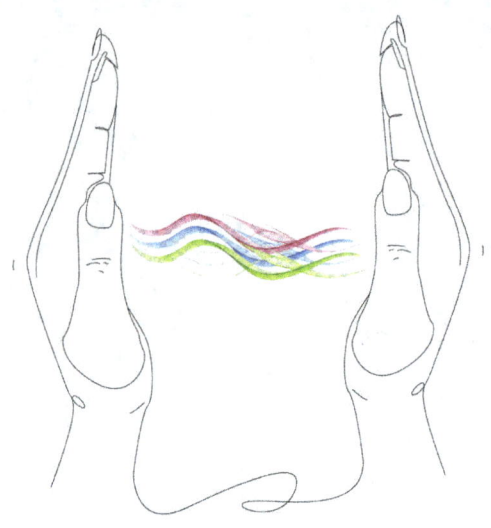

sometimes,
you have to be stingy
with your energy;
you are not for everyone
everyone is not for you
...and that is okay.

picky.

the unapologetic introvert;
stands in a crowd
riddled with conformists,
yearning for isolation
while content with her perceived loneliness.

withdrawn.

i solemnly swear
to love myself;
despite the instagram glorified ideologies
of desirable female bodies.

21st century oath.

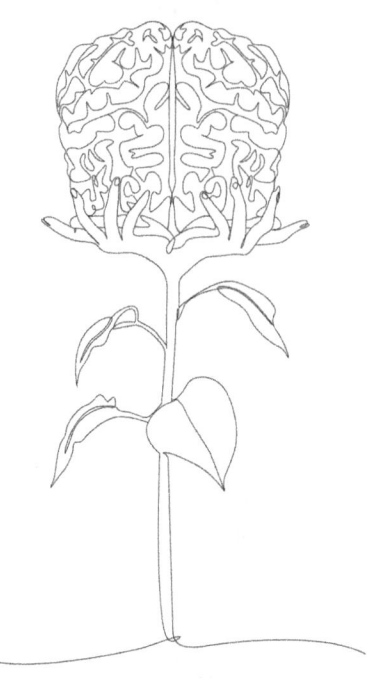

nourish the surroundings
of the environment you inhabit;
with knowledge of the merely simplistic,
the complexly explainable,
and the profound comprehension
of self-love.

intellectual growth.

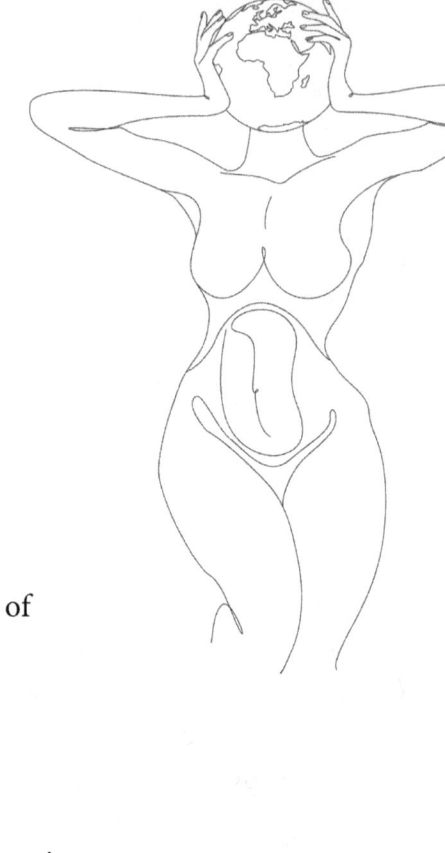

bear witness;
to the combination
of phenotypes
from two young lovers of
african descent.
her coiled roots
big lips
big booty
wide hips
skin pigment resembling cinnamon;
are the end result
of the union
between an afro-guyanese
and cameroonian.

the author's self-admiration.

exist in a world
where PERFECTION
is just a configuration
of six consonants and four vowels.

merely a group of letters.

they would never see
the most beautiful
part of me,
until they read
my poetry.

*i enjoyed sharing and i hope
you enjoyed reading.*

Dear reader, if you have made it this far, I would like to thank you so much for taking the time out to experience what I feel is my…gift. Poetry can be subjective; thus, the words you read may have been perceived differently than what I may have intended. While your thoughts and feelings are fresh, I would love if on the next couple of pages, you could write down what these words may have done for you. If you have to re-read the chapters in order to provide more details of your emotional experiences, I welcome you to do that.

What Lays Beneath My Shade

What Lays Beneath My Shade

What Lays Beneath My Shade

What Lays Beneath My Shade

These notes are not for you to share…unless you want to! As someone who spends a lot of time in my head and often makes notes on things that weigh on my heart, it is therapeutic not only to write, but to later stumble upon what I wrote in the past. With this, I am able to acknowledge the evolution of my thought processes. You might read this book again and have a totally different experience dependent on what may be taking place in your life.

I'd also like to share that inadvertently, there were themes amongst these poems that allowed me to group them together into mini chapters. Compiling them into a book was nerve-racking and fun; like putting together a puzzle, since they were all written at very random times in my life. My hope is for every reader to gravitate to at least one poem—no matter how melancholy the subject matter might be. Be patient with your mind, and I hope to grace your thought processes again in the future <3

Lastly, I would like to give the biggest thank you to the kindhearted Olga (Lola) Fedorets, not only for the illustrations of the front and back cover, but for a few illustrations inside of the book and for providing the inspiration for other images as well. I would like to thank God and all of my ancestors for making my existence possible through the union of my loving parents. Thank you to my family and friends for being as supportive as they could, even though the writing of this book was kept a secret from most of them lol. And thank you to a special someone for investing love—not only into me, but into my dream of completing this long overdue book.

THANK YOU.

www.ingramcontent.com/pod-product-compliance
Lightning Source LLC
Chambersburg PA
CBHW070937080526
44589CB00013B/1537